D0055782

LEADING WOMEN

Queen Latifah

Award-
Winning
Actress and
Hip-Hop
Activist

AMY PETTINELLA

Cavendish
Square

New York

Published in 2015 by Cavendish Square Publishing, LLC
243 5th Avenue, Suite 136, New York, NY 10016

Library of Congress Cataloging-in-Publication Data

Pettinella, Amy.
Queen Latifah : award-winning actress and hip-hop activist / Amy Pettinella.
pages cm. — (Leading women)
Includes bibliographical references and index.
ISBN 978-1-62712-984-8 (hardcover) ISBN 978-1-62712-986-2 (ebook)
1. Queen Latifah, 1970—Juvenile literature. 2. Rap musicians—United States—Biography—
Juvenile literature. 3. Television actors and actresses—United States—Biography—Juvenile literature.
4. Motion picture actors and actresses—United States—Biography—
Juvenile literature. I. Title.
ML3930.L178P47 2014
782.421649092—dc23
[B]
2014005324

Editorial Director: Dean Miller
Editor: Andrew Coddington
Copy Editor: Michele Suchomel-Casey
Art Director: Jeffrey Talbot
Designer: Amy Greenan/Joseph Macri
Photo Researcher: J8 Media
Production Manager: Jennifer Ryder-Talbot
Production Editor: David McNamara

CONTENTS

CHAPTER ONE

Destined for Royalty

Her journey could best be described as an odyssey. From the little girl in apartment 3K of the Hyatt Court **housing projects** to the multimillionaire media mogul with her own star on Hollywood Boulevard, Dana Owens has been a fiery force of nature since the day she was born.

"From the very beginning, I knew my daughter was going to be different," Rita Bray Owens said of her daughter, Dana Elaine Owens, who would one day be known to the world as Queen Latifah. Born in Newark, New Jersey, on March 18, 1970, three weeks after her due date, her mother said, "I finally had to tell the doctors to go in and get her. And she fought them, too. She was eight pounds, three ounces, with a mind all her own from day one." Dana would keep that fiery attitude throughout her life, making a name for herself as a musician, an actress, a **producer**, and an activist for race, gender, and sexual orientation equality.

Extraordinary Expectations

Carving out your own brand of royalty isn't easy, and Dana gives her parents much of the credit for the strength her "subjects" so admire. Who were the people who raised Queen Latifah? It turns out they were just ordinary people who happened to have extraordinary expectations.

Dana was the second child of Lancelot "Lance" Owens, Sr. and Rita Bray Owens. Rita grew up in the South, the middle daughter of seven children. Her father was a sergeant in the army, and her mother came from a long line of housekeepers. Rita's parents were loving and encouraging but very strict. Socializing was limited to school, church, and family gatherings. The children were all expected to do very well in school, and if they ever came home with no homework, their father would give them homework of his own devising and send them to the library. The Brays wanted their children to have opportunities they never had, and raised them to be smart, strong, and respectful of others and themselves.

Early on, Rita's parents could see she was different and tended toward shyness, which was made worse by the many moves her family had to make while her father was in the army. Noting she was artistically inclined, they tried their best in difficult financial circumstances to nurture her sensibilities. Birthday and Christmas presents were usually some sort of paints and brushes, which Rita received with delight. When he wrote her letters from overseas, her father would always include drawings of places he'd seen. Rita treasured these letters her entire life and took them as a sign that he was encouraging her artistic interests.

Rita's tight-knit family gave her structure and security but kept her somewhat sheltered from the harsh realities of life in the South in the 1950s. Even though she attended a segregated school, she didn't experience racism until she was eleven years old. On that life-changing day, she was walking alone to a neighborhood pool when a car full of white boys drove past her, slowed down, rolled down the windows, and yelled, "Go home, n-----!"

Terrified, she ran home and cried to her father, who dried her tears. He told her that there were two kinds of people in the world: the ignorant and the enlightened. Although it pained him to tell her that people would judge and hate her because of her skin color, he felt a responsibility to arm her with knowledge, wisdom, and courage. From that day on, he instilled in her that she must rise above such language and abuse and not let it infect her with fear or hatred.

When Rita was sixteen, she had been accepted to both Howard University and Spelman College. However one night she was invited to be a backup singer at the

Jim Crow Laws

Although slavery had been abolished (outlawed) in 1865 in the United States, African Americans faced a harsh life, fraught with discrimination, racism, and outright violence throughout the twentieth century and even today. Life in the South in particular, where Rita Bray Owens grew up, was inhospitable, unfair, and sometimes dangerous for black citizens, due in part to the **Jim Crow laws.**

The Jim Crow laws were a form of legalized segregation, in which black citizens were denied basic civil rights, such as the right to vote or own property, and access to suitable housing, transportation, employment, education, and medicine. The laws were designed to demoralize black citizens and to ensure their continued low status in the social hierarchy of the day. Because black citizens were denied a proper education, many were not able to advance in careers and continued to live in poverty as sharecroppers and domestic servants.

In addition to discrimination, black citizens were also systematically harassed and terrorized by white racist groups such as the **Ku Klux Klan (KKK)**. These groups were typically protected by corrupt law enforcement officials. Terrorist acts included kidnapping, beating, torture, hanging effigies (a distasteful crude likeness of someone often in the form of a scarecrow), and, placing burning crosses at residences of black citizens or their sympathizers. Racism was not relegated to the South. In the North, many black citizens were denied bank loans to purchase homes, admission to colleges and social groups, and career opportunities.

service club on the army base. Rita loved singing, but was nervous—a very handsome man with whom she had locked eyes earlier that evening was in the band. That handsome young man turned out to be a soldier named Lancelot Owens. He was in the Honor Guard and fresh off a tour of duty in Vietnam.

It was love at first sight for both Rita and Lance, and within a year they were married and expecting their first child. Despite being married and pregnant by age seventeen, Rita managed to earn her high school diploma. Smitten with her new husband and determined to be a good mother, she gave up her chance to attend college, a decision that would affect her later in life. A sheltered country girl her whole life, she was suddenly married to a worldly man and living in a big city up north—his hometown of Newark, New Jersey. Although she felt overwhelmed, she had plenty of help from Lance's mother and sister, who helped her set up her home and navigate life in a busy northern city.

Two years after Dana was born, her brother, Lancelot Jr., joined the family. As a baby, Lance Jr. often kept his eyes shut tight even when awake, which made him look as if he was winking. His parents started calling him "Winki," and the name stuck.

Anything a Boy Can Do...

Building their children's emotional and physical strength was imperative to Rita and Lance. When Dana and Winki were both babies, Rita began writing letters to them, recounting the joy of watching them grow. Although she always felt loved by her own parents, she was one of seven children, and personal interaction with her mother was limited, which sometimes left Rita feeling lonely. She wanted her own children to grow up knowing that they were not only loved but also cherished and that they could come to her for anything. Those letters are treasured by Dana as an adult, and are a sustaining force that remind her of her family's unconditional love.

Unlike most parents of Rita's background, she encouraged her children to ask questions, challenge decisions, and voice their opinions. In doing so, she was teaching them how to challenge authority respectfully and to learn how good decisions are made. Whether she knew it or not, Rita was putting everything in place for her children to grow up with strong hearts and minds.

Lance was the perfect parental complement to Rita. While Rita nurtured their children's hearts, Lance nurtured their sense of adventure. He wanted them to be physically and mentally strong so they could handle the pressures of a ruthless world and not suffer at the hands of bullies and users. He believed that teaching them from an early age to stand up to adversity and difficulty would build their character and give them confidence.

Looking back, Queen Latifah is grateful for her father's beliefs, which were considered very progressive for a man of his generation. Firmly believing in equality, he encouraged Dana to participate in all manner of physical activities that were largely thought of as boys' play. When Winki wanted to play football, basketball, or baseball with his father, Dana would be invited to play, too. When Winki expressed an interest in learning karate, their father also enrolled Dana in classes. At first, Rita feared that playing roughly with boys would damage Dana's sweet sensibilities, but once she saw how much she loved athletics, she allowed her daugher to pursue whatever sport she wished. Despite her vulnerable heart, Dana had a fierce competitive streak, which Rita knew would one day serve her well.

The concrete jungle of Newark was a tough place to grow up, and Lance wanted his children to experience and respect nature. Having been trained to survive in the jungles of Vietnam, Lance believed that learning basic survival skills would give his children not only physical strength but wisdom and patience. He loved to take Dana and Winki on camping trips, where he taught them to scout trails, use a compass, build fires, catch fish, cook outdoors, and pitch tents. Dana recalls the nights of cooking over an open fire and sleeping under the stars with her brother and father as some of the happiest in her life. It was on one of these trips that her father told her,

> *"Dana, just because you're a girl don't ever let anybody tell you that you can't. I know you can!"*

A decorated soldier and police officer, Lance felt it was his responsibility to teach his children to handle and respect firearms because he had to carry one for work. Going to shooting ranges became a favorite pastime for Lance and his children, and both Dana and Winki became sharpshooters. Shooting was not a sport that most girls were interested in, but Dana loved the challenge—and knowing that her father trusted and respected her. It was all part of Lance's plan to assure his daughter that she could do anything a boy could do.

Family Life

As far as Dana and Winki were concerned, they had the perfect life. Dana was very proud of her parents, who had a loving relationship with their children and with each other. Lance and Rita Owens were very stylish, and Dana loved the attention and respect they commanded on the street.

Lance moved up the ladder on the police squad, and Rita eventually found work as a secretary. With two incomes, plenty of ambition, and a desire to give their children the best life had to offer, the Owens family embarked on a life of slow but steady upward **social mobility.** Every two years or so, the family would move into a nicer apartment in a better neighborhood, and it was an exciting time for all of them.

Thursday nights were always a favorite for the Owens family because Thursday was payday for Lance. The family would get dressed up and go to a nice Chinese restaurant and then to a movie. After the movie, they'd often drive to upscale neighborhoods and dream about the house they'd have someday.

The Owens family lived in several of Newark's neighborhoods, including places similar to this middle-class one.

One night when there were driving home from one of their excursions, they drove past a rough street corner and noticed a man slapping a woman. Unfortunately, these scenes were common in their neighborhood, but Dana could not stomach the sight of the woman being battered by a man. She begged her father to stop it. With that, Lance stopped the car, got out, and accosted the man. The woman ran off, and Lance lectured the abusive man. In doing this, he sent a powerful message to his daughter: Don't ever tolerate abuse.

Rita and Lance didn't have a lot of money, but they had a lot of imagination and gave their children fond memories of growing up. Sometimes, they'd pack up a feast in a picnic basket, go to a park, and pretend they were in the wilderness. In the summer, they'd make a day of driving to the Jersey shore and playing on the beach and the boardwalk. Instead of eating out, Rita would pack a basket of homemade fried chicken and a gallon of Kool-Aid, and they feasted like kings.

The best times, however, happened right in their own living room, where there was always music playing. Her parents were both singers, so it was no surprise when Dana also took to singing. Rita and Lance loved to get dressed up and entertain guests in their home, and that meant one thing: music and dancing. Dana loved to put on concerts for the party guests, singing along with the likes of Aretha Franklin, Luther Vandross, and Earth, Wind & Fire.

In addition to enjoying the good things in life, Rita and Lance felt strongly about their children's education. After dinner every night, Mr. and Mrs. Owens would make Dana and Winki read various articles from the newspaper aloud. If they ever came to a word they couldn't pronounce, they would be sent to the dictionary. Dana and Winki impressed their parents by using complex words in conversation, and their efforts were rewarded with rich praise from both parents, which was more valuable than gold.

Queen Latifah loves having her family close by when she is on the road. They remind her of who she is when fame becomes overwhelming.

When Dana was in grade school, she tested as intellectually gifted. Upon learning this, Rita enrolled both Dana and Winki in a private Catholic school. Knowing that tuition would be a financial strain on the family's finances, Dana and Winki worked hard in school to ensure the investment in their education wasn't wasted.

The Legacy Begins

Starting a new school was tough on Dana. The other kids had been together since kindergarten, and they did not take kindly to Dana's athletic prowess. Despite being tough on the outside, she was very tender and sensitive on the inside. She was always the tallest one in her class, which made her self-conscious of her appearance. Boys taunted her constantly, calling her "tomboy," and Dana knew the name was meant to hurt her.

"They were saying straight out that I somehow wanted to be a boy and that I wasn't pretty or cute the way a regular girl should be."

Her mother assured Dana that the boys were simply fearful that she was a better athlete than they were. She offered her daughter a rebuttal:

When Dana tried it out, she received baffled looks at first, but standing up to her bullies made her feel better than letting them harass her and define her. The teasing stopped soon enough, and before she knew it, she was being picked first for every team at recess and in gym class.

At only nine years old, Dana had made a life decision: She would never let anyone define her or tell her what she could and couldn't do. She had no idea that, ten years later, she would personally turn the world's notion of what girls could and couldn't do upside-down.

CHAPTER TWO

"Latifah" Is Born

The dinner table was the heart and soul of the Owens family. Winki and Dana were encouraged to participate in conversations about current events and politics, especially when those events affected black people. The 1960s and '70s were turbulent decades in American history, and riots became commonplace as a reaction to violent racism. Newark was a city that was spinning out of control, as the disenfranchised black population scrambled for housing and employment and was met with backlash from employers, landlords, and others.

Lance was interested in the **Black Power** movement of the 1960s, which some believe polarized the

civil rights movement. "Black Power" was a term that described the political struggles and victories of black people in an oppressive society. The Black Power movement had many factions, with some sides demanding peaceful negotiations, such as the followers of Martin Luther King, Jr., and other sides believing that the only way to fight violence was with violence, such as followers of Stokely Carmichael and Malcolm X. Lance felt strongly that his children should understand the obstacles they could face in society because of the color of their skin, and he presented them with the many sides of racism and how people fought it.

Apartheid—the government-sanctioned segregation of black people in South Africa—was another form of extreme racism that came to a boiling point while Dana was growing up. Dana and her mother often discussed how this violent regime affected women in particular. With so much negativity surrounding the black experience, Rita felt it just as important to share stories of victory with Dana, and she regaled her with stories of ancient African queens, such as Queen Nefertiti of Egypt and Queen Amina of Zaria. Just as Rita hoped, Dana chose to gravitate toward these strong women, rulers of strong civilizations and armies, and began to see them as her ancestors. At the time, Rita had no idea just how profound these conversations were to Dana.

In the wake of racism run amok, it was common for black people to rename themselves with titles they felt

more accurately reflected their ancestral identity. Some
famous African Americans who changed their names
included champion boxer Muhammad Ali, who was
previously know as Cassius Clay, and civil rights leader
Malcolm X, who dropped his surname Little (what many
referred to as his "slave name") as a means of protest
to the suffering of black citizens at the hands of white
racists. Dana described the practice this way:

*"People were looking for a sense of self that
went beyond what they thought society had
to offer."*

When Dana was eight years old, she and her
cousin Sharonda decided to choose African names for
themselves, as many of their peers had already done.
Sharonda chose "Salima," and Dana chose "Latifah."
She liked the lyrical sound of it, pronouncing it with the
emphasis on the "La" syllable. (LA-ti-fah). Moreover,
she liked the meaning: "delicate, sensitive, and kind." On
the outside, Dana knew she came across as somewhat
formidable, and she felt that people had no idea that on
the inside she was quite the opposite.

Leading Activist: Malcolm X

Malcolm X, born Malcolm Little, in Omaha, Nebraska, in 1925, was a leading civil rights activist and is considered one of the most influential people in U.S. history. He grew up the son of a Baptist minister who openly spoke against racism, and as a result, was constantly harassed and threatened by the KKK. The family relocated to Lansing, Michigan, where his father was brutally murdered by The Black Legion, a white supremacist group with ties to the KKK. The Black Legion was absolved of the crime. X's mother subsequently had a nervous breakdown, leaving X effectively orphaned. He quit school in the eighth grade and partook of a life of petty crime until he landed in jail at the age of twenty-one.

While serving his prison sentence, he began following the Black Muslims, a political-religious group who openly spurned racism and encouraged black citizens to rise up against their aggressors. Once released from prison, X renounced his former life of crime and eventually became a leading activist and gifted orator in the American civil rights movement. Some considered his teachings to have a polarizing effect on the movement because his beliefs contrasted with those of civil rights leader Dr. Martin Luther King, Jr. While King believed that peace was the only answer to violence, Malcolm X believed that violence was an appropriate response to violence. Many people who supported the civil rights movement found truth in his harsh words. Soon, Malcolm X's widespread singular popularity spurned jealousy within the Black Muslims.

Disillusioned with what he considered to be some hypocritical actions, X left the Black Muslims and traveled to Mecca in Saudi Arabia in 1964, seeking enlightenment, after which he changed his name to el-Hajj Malik el-Shabazz. Upon his return, his views on violence had changed drastically, and he ultimately believed that revolution should be achieved peacefully. His actions outraged the Black Muslims, who, in retaliation, assassinated Malcolm X in 1965, an event he had predicted some time earlier. His **posthumous** publication *The Autobiography of Malcolm X* is considered by many to be one of the finest works of literature in American history for its unflinching account of history and the author's uncanny ability to point out his own shortcomings and wrongdoings.

> *"I loved the meaning and I loved how it made me feel—feminine and special. I knew who I was inside, and I wanted to show a bit of that on the outside—with my name."*

What "Latifah" really meant to Dana was freedom. Choosing her own identity was her first step in defining who she was outside of being a daughter, a sister, or a girl from "around the way." Although people still called her "Dana," her close friends and family understood what her chosen name meant to her and called her "Latifah," or "La" for short. Although she was a young girl at the time, Latifah was already beginning to make her mark on the world.

Big Changes for the Owens Family

In 1978, the family lived in a comfortable and spacious garden apartment in a middle class neighborhood of Newark called Hillside. One night, Rita and Lance called Dana and Winki into the living room and broke the news that they would be separating. Dana was shocked. She rarely heard her parents fight or even raise their voices, and they had always been a very close family. Dana didn't understand why her father couldn't live with them anymore and why they had to leave their beautiful apartment. Her perfect world was shattered, and life changed forever from that moment on.

Unlike many couples who divorce, Rita and Lance did not partake in name calling or complaining about each other to their children. Dana was very grateful that her parents spared them further misery and taught them that mutual respect is the most important thing for a family, even if the family had separated.

Little by little, Rita began to share with her children the reason for their separation. Lance was a loving father and good provider, but he suffered untold emotional damage as a soldier in Vietnam and as a police officer on the violent streets of Newark. His line of work sometimes required him to kill people, and the guilt became overwhelming. A proud and perhaps stubborn man, he didn't seek psychological advice to help him process and relieve his guilt. Instead, he turned to drugs and extramarital affairs to help him ease his pain.

His actions hurt and betrayed Rita, and although she still loved him, she knew she had to leave. She didn't want Dana to believe that women had no choice but to tolerate unfaithfulness, and she didn't want Winki to believe that husbands were not required to be faithful to their wives. She also didn't want her children to be exposed to the erratic and irresponsible behaviors of a drug abuser.

For the first time in her life, Rita was about to be truly on her own, only now she had two young children to raise. Her first decision was to get the college degree she gave up ten years earlier to get married. With a college degree, she could get a better job and be a better provider for her children. Most importantly, she wanted to set an example of determination for her children. She had just suffered a serious blow from the man who stole her heart, but she resolved to start over and have the life she had always dreamed of having.

Life in 3K

Rita didn't make much money, and as a result, she and the children temporarily moved to a housing project called Hyatt Court. Dana and Winki had grown accustomed to moving up in the world, but moving to the brick and mortar square building of Hyatt Court was a huge step down. Rita assured them that it was a temporary move, and worked two and sometimes three jobs to ensure they could stay in private school.

Living in Hyatt Court was an education for Dana and Winki, who had known only a middle-class lifestyle. Rita did her best to explain the living conditions at Hyatt Court. Some people, like themselves, were there temporarily until circumstances improved and they could afford private housing. Others who lived there seemed completely resigned to staying, which prevented them from ever doing anything meaningful with their lives. Although there were some friendly people, Rita feared that the negativity, lack of ambition, and most of all lack of consideration for other residents would affect her children.

To combat the negativity that permeated the halls of

Hyatt Court, Rita created a clean, warm, and personal living space. With very little money, she managed to put personal touches on their otherwise barren apartment, and the focal point was the dining room. Every night they would eat together as a family and say a prayer of gratitude for all that they had.

At first Dana was fascinated by life in the projects. She'd never been surrounded by so many people and so much activity. Her bedroom overlooked the courtyard, where people from the three buildings often congregated. Whatever was happening in the courtyard, Rita forbid Dana and Winki from joining. Rita knew that the courtyard was where drug deals were made and children slacked off instead of going to school.

She sent them to a nearby community center where they could play safely and under the supervision of adults. When Rita learned that the community center offered low-cost music lessons, she enrolled them both in guitar class.

Although they had a safe and happy life inside the walls of their apartment, Rita and the children encountered hostility and verbal abuse from the other residents. They made fun of Dana and Winki for going to private school, and they accused Rita of snobbery because she went to college, dressed up for work, and spoke with a proper southern **dialect** instead of using slang. Still, Rita was determined to make the best of things and to get the most out of their time there. It bothered Rita to see children with no exposure to the greater things life had to offer, and she'd sometimes organize field trips for children and parents in the building to the Bronx Zoo, the Jersey shore, and area parks.

In the summer months, Rita sent Dana and Winki to stay with relatives in the country in Maryland and Virginia so that they could play outside and be surrounded by positive people who loved them and wanted the best for them. It was here that Dana started attending church, and where she loved singing in the choir. Being in the country made Dana and Winki feel

Surrounded by family and loved ones, Dana received a star on the Hollywood Walk of Fame.

young, alive, and free. They missed the camping trips they used to take with their father, and being able to play outside day and night reminded them how much they loved nature.

Unfortunately, conditions worsened when they returned to Hyatt Park. At Christmas, Rita took on extra hours at work so she could buy Dana and Winki gifts, which she wrapped and hid in the trunk of her car. Someone in the building must have been watching her, however—her car was burglarized on Christmas Eve and all the gifts were stolen. This was a heartbreaking blow for Rita, who was looking forward to surprising her children with new toys and clothes. More than ever, she was determined to get her family out of the projects within a year.

On weekends, Rita and the children would drive through neighborhoods and look at houses. When they had found the perfect house, Rita went to the bank, down payment in hand, to apply for a mortgage loan. Sadly, in the early 1980s, banks rarely gave loans to women, especially single women of color. Dana, even though she was just a little girl, took note of how minorities and women were treated in society. She knew her life would be a constant uphill battle, but she resolved to fight it with determination and grace, just like her mother had.

An Exodus

Keeping her promise to move out of the projects, Rita instead found a three-family home to rent. The family said their good-byes to friends they had made at Hyatt Court, but disaster was about to strike again. While the kids were at school and Rita was at work, a moving van showed up and packed up all their things—only Rita didn't hire this moving company. In a single afternoon, someone had stolen everything they owned.

Always brave and calm under pressure, Rita didn't allow the children to shed tears for the things they lost. She encouraged them to focus on their new life instead. Their new house on Littleton Avenue had three floors, with a different family living on each floor. The rooms were spacious and airy, and best of all, they now had a huge backyard full of trees. Dana and Winki felt happy, safe, and comfortable in their new house, and they would spend the majority of their adolescence living here.

All that was missing in Dana's heart and mind was her father. Rita had recently broken the news that they would be getting formally divorced. Dana's heart broke, and even though she loved her mother, she didn't understand why she couldn't reunite with their father. Rita felt she had no choice but to tell her children the truth: While she and Lance Sr. were married, he'd had affairs with other women and fathered children with them. He had been living a double life.

Dana and Winki now felt the betrayal that their mother felt, and for a number of years, they lost contact with their father. This was a very difficult and confusing time for Dana. She had lost the most important man in her life and began to question everything. Not even a teenager yet, Dana began to search her soul for answers. How could the man who gave her such happy memories and a sound upbringing have done such a thing to his family?

Eventually Dana learned to focus on the good things in her life, such as the love that surrounded her, and this gave her incredible strength and wisdom. She learned early on that the only thing she could control in life was how she chose to live it. She grew up fast the day she learned this. It marked her **exodus** from childhood, and she faced the future bravely.

CHAPTER THREE

The Irvington Years

Life was good on Littleton Avenue. Dana and Winki made friends in the neighborhood, and Rita's parents often came up from Virginia for long visits. Rita continued her studies at Kean College and often took Dana and Winki to night school with her. The two had befriended the college janitor and loved accompanying her on her rounds and helping her with her duties. Rita felt good knowing that her children were being exposed to hard-working people, both working class and those hoping for a higher education.

Money was as tight as ever, but Dana's mother still found ways to take them to museums, musicals, and music events. She also filled their house with art and literature magazines so that they would be constantly surrounded by the good things in life. Rita was determined to show her children that they could have the best life had to offer if they worked hard.

Through the various moves and changes in their family, Dana and Winki grew very close. When they lived in the projects, Rita didn't want them hanging around the courtyard, which meant that they had to hang out together doing other things. Unlike most brothers and sisters, they were very close friends. They had their moments of bickering, but their parents had done a good job of teaching family bonding, and they had a deep respect for one another.

When they moved to Littleton Avenue, Winki took on the role of "man of the house." He got a part-time job to help his mother with household expenses, and he even gave Dana a $10 weekly allowance to do his laundry and clean his room. In the early 1980s, a $10 allowance was considered a windfall, and Dana delighted in earning money for herself. Rita was proud of her children, who exhibited a strong work ethic.

After years of diligence, Rita graduated from college, and she fulfilled her lifelong dream of becoming an art teacher. She was hired by nearby Irvington High School, which Dana and Winki both eventually attended. Some high school kids would be horrified to go to school where their mother worked, but not Winki and Dana. Their mom, known around Irvington High as "Ms. O," was a popular and respected member of faculty.

Ms. O. had a special gift for taking at-risk kids who needed extra attention under her wing, and they would thrive under her guidance. Ms. O also started a popular after-school program that gave kids an escape from the violent and troubled streets of Newark. The program offered teenagers an environment safe from negative peer pressure, where they could paint, sing, put on plays, and talk openly about their fears and dreams. The program was so successful that Ms. O. received a governor's award for her efforts.

Dana was busy leading her own life, but watching her mother make a positive difference in the lives of troubled kids had a tremendous impact on her. She began to wonder how she could do something worthwhile in the world. Dana was great at sports and singing and was well liked by the student body, but she had the unshakable feeling that the world had a bigger calling for her.

Forgiveness and Forging On

Dana's thoughts often turned to her father, from whom she had become estranged after learning about his infidelities. As she grew up, she experienced a lot of success in school, and she knew that at least part of that success was due to the attention her father gave her as a young girl. She was still very angry with him, yet she couldn't deny how much she loved him.

Even though they were divorced, Lance still looked out for his family. When a man began stalking Rita, hoping to date her, Lance confronted the man and made sure he never bothered his family again. Actions like that made it impossible for Dana to think that her father didn't love them. A heartfelt talk with a close friend and an aunt who had both lost their fathers made Dana realize that she wanted to forgive her father and have him in her life.

He had been a tremendous influence on her, and it hurt more to punish him by keeping away than to forgive him. Forgiving him proved to heal her from past hurts. She felt stronger and was convinced that life is about choices—what you do with it and what you choose to remember. Dana chose to remember the good. This early decision to have a positive attitude would have a major impact on her future singing career, which was just a few years down the road.

The Star of Irvington High

Her first year at Irvington, Dana signed up for the talent show despite not knowing a soul in the audience besides her brother. She walked onstage, hoping no one could see her trembling, and took the microphone. As she started out the opening measures of Luther Vandross' "If Only for One Night," she caught the eye of someone in the audience who encouraged her with a nod. As her confidence grew, she let the passion of the song overtake her, and the audience thundered with appreciation.

Dana was a gifted student and was so advanced that she skipped a grade. Being the youngest in her class did not daunt her. Classmates flocked to this force of nature whom some people called "Latifah." In addition to being a star pupil and a star in the school play, Dana was also a star basketball player. Twice she helped her team get to the state finals, winning the championship in 1984. It was on the court that she met her lifelong best friend "Slammin' Jammin'" Tammy Hammond.

New Friends

Being confident and positive herself, Dana wanted to attract confident and positive people. She sought out friendships with people whom she felt would inspire her and hold her accountable. She had no interest in people who just wanted to ride her coattails and flatter her. It seemed everyone loved Dana, but one boy in particular, Shawn "Shakim" Compere, took a liking to her and had the guts to tell her so. Dana was flattered, but Shakim's bad habits troubled her. He smoked, cut class, and seemed to have no direction in life. Accustomed to ambitious people, Dana gently told him that she couldn't date someone who didn't respect himself. Hoping to win her affections, he gave up smoking, started studying, and eventually outshone Dana in the classroom. During this transition, they developed a deep friendship based on trust and respect. He was grateful to Dana for encouraging him to reach higher in life, and one day soon, he would find a way to repay her for her honesty and friendship.

Dana had an ease with boys that most girls her age seemed to lack. She liked to hang out and play basketball and listen to **hip-hop** music, and boys found her to be more down-to-earth than other girls. Around school, she kept hearing about a guy called Ramsey and was dying to meet him. He was nineteen, had recently emigrated from Liberia, and had his own apartment. Dana finally met this mystery man by the football field one day. They became fast friends and were practically inseparable. Ramsey's worldliness fascinated Dana. He knew music better than anyone thanks to his numerous forays into New York City, where hip-hop clubs were all the rage, and he shared all the latest music with her. He also had a reputation for being a style icon, which also impressed Dana, as she felt that creating a distinct image was important to one's success.

Growing Pains

Knowing that her daughter was an excellent student and disciplined athlete, Rita never expected to have trouble with Dana. From the time she was a little girl, she taught her to openly express her questions, fears, and desires, believing that good communication is the backbone of good relationships. As far as she could tell, all was well with Dana. One night, however, Rita awoke to find Dana missing from her bedroom. She called all of her friends and relatives, but no one knew where she was. Next, she called all the area hospitals, but still no luck. This was

The Hip-hop Movement

DJ Cool Herc (Clive Campbell) is considered the grandfather of the Hip-hop Movement, where he began spinning records and sampling songs in 1973 in the South Bronx, a borough of the city of New York. Herc is credited with bringing the Jamaican music known as reggae to the U.S., which went on to inspire rap music. Hip-hop contains four pillars of culture, including graffiti, a form of self-expression of the inner city experience; DJing, or disc jockeying, in which recordings are played and sampled in clubs and house parties; B-Boying, also known as break dancing; and Emceeing, which is another name for rapping.

The Hip-hop Movement became prevalent in the 1980s, and some say was that generation's answer to the stalled civil rights movement of the 1960s and 1970s. Although it is most associated with the struggles and achievements of the black population, hip-hop encompasses the artistic expressions of many ethnicities, including Hispanic, West Indian, African, and white, which has greatly contributed to its widespread popularity. Jeff Chang, the award-winning author of *Can't Stop Won't Stop: A History of the Hip-Hop Generation*, has characterized the importance of the 40-year old Hip-hop Movement as thus: "I believe in the values that have sustained hip-hop from the beginning: inclusion, recognition, creativity, and transformation. In the end, hip-hop is about teenagers, it's about youth. And as long as they are taking those values forward, hip-hop won't die."

long before cell phones, so tracking her down personally was nearly impossible. Fraught with worry, Rita and Winki paced the floors all night and called the police. Early the next morning, Dana attempted to sneak in the front door. Winki accosted her immediately, and Dana knew she was in big trouble.

It turned out that Dana had been sneaking out for weeks and returning in the small hours of the morning. Rita was devastated, but mostly confused. Dana had always been a child who hated to disappoint people, especially her mother, and with their open communication style, Rita had hoped her children would never feel the need to be dishonest.

Dana was doing well in school and in basketball, and she even held down a part-time job at Burger King. Why did she feel the need to jeopardize her success, and where on earth was she going? The answer horrified Rita: Dana had been sneaking out with Ramsey and Shakim and going to hip-hop clubs in Times Square in New York City. Worse, there were times she would sneak into the city alone, which was a potentially dangerous thing to do. Times Square in the mid-1980s was hardly the family-friendly place it is today. Back then it was filled with strip joints, pawn shops, shady movie theaters, drug dealers, and gang fights. It was no place for a teenage girl to be on her own.

It took a while, but Dana was finally able to communicate to her mother the draw that rap music and the hip-hop culture had on her. She loved everything about her life, but when she was at these clubs, dancing and being part of the culture, she felt something stir deep inside of her that she couldn't explain. She just knew that it was the most important thing in her life, and she'd do anything to stay involved with the **scene**. Hip-hop had not yet made it to New Jersey clubs, so going to New York was her only option.

As Rita took in everything Dana was saying, she tried to bite her tongue. She knew that if she downplayed the significance of hip-hop culture Dana would feel slighted. Looking back, she had to accept that she encouraged Dana to be her own person her entire life, and now that she was growing up, she would be even more assertive in her beliefs. Rita didn't understand it herself, but she began to recognize just how important this new culture was to Dana. She remembered that Dana had been an obedient and respectful child her whole life. Whatever pull these hip-hop clubs had on her daughter, Rita wanted Dana to know that above all she trusted her to make smart decisions about her safety and the company she kept. They agreed on some ground rules, namely that Dana would never again lie, sneak out, or go to the city alone. This period was an exciting time for Dana but a scary time for Rita, who knew she had no choice but to exercise her faith and trust her daughter.

The Latin Quarter

The Latin Quarter nightclub in Times Square was the **mecca** of the hip-hop movement. Onstage were the best rhymers and rappers, and in the audience were the best dancers. Hip-hop was a culture all its own, and Dana immersed herself fully. On Saturdays, her friends would meet her at Burger King when she got off her shift. She'd run to the bathroom, change out of her uniform, and throw on a designer sweat suit, which was the fashion then. The Latin Quarter attracted the best talent:

The now-fabled Latin Quarter, where Dana spent countless hours honing her skills, was located in New York City's Times Square.

Run-DMC, Kool Moe Dee, LL Kool J, and Grand Master Flash all made appearances on its stage.

Dana was in the crowd the first time the female rap duo Salt-N-Pepa took the stage and brought down the house. Female **MCs** (hip-hop slang for rappers, short for "master of ceremonies") were almost unheard of at the time, and Dana was floored. It wasn't until a female duo named Sweet T and Jazzy Joyce took the stage, however, that Dana started harboring dreams about being a rapper herself. Sweet T and Jazzy Joyce were the first female rappers with whom Dana felt she could identify. They dressed like her, in sweat suits, and flaunted their strength and grit instead of their sexuality. The audience went wild over their performance, and Dana was encouraged that people could appreciate women for more than their sex appeal and listen to what they had to say. Dana was a young woman with a lot to say, and rap became her platform.

Unfortunately, the club started getting a bad reputation due to gang fights and was finally torn down in the late 1980s—but not before Dana would perform there herself. Of course, she didn't perform under the name Dana Owens. By that time, Dana was performing under a much more royal moniker.

During her early trips to the Latin Quarter, Queen Latifah made connections with many young rappers, including Jaz-O (left) and Jay-Z (right).

CHAPTER FOUR

A True Calling

Although Rita was never completely comfortable with Dana's forays into Manhattan, she held tight to her faith that she would be safe. She had never seen Dana so taken with anything, and it seemed that hip-hop was more than a passing interest. Dana was different when she talked about being a part of the scene and bringing that scene back to "Jersey."

Madison and Stuyvesant: Jersey's Rap Central

Rita had been put in charge of organizing school dances, which put her in touch with a DJ named Mark the 45 King. Mark was from the Bronx, a borough of New York City considered to be the birthplace of rap, and had done extensive work on the record turntables with many notable rappers. Mark had recently moved to Irvington near the corner of

Madison and Stuyvesant, the area eventually referred to as Jersey's Rap Central, and Rita thought he would be a good contact for Dana.

Mark turned out to be more than a good contact. He and Dana became fast friends, and he introduced her to his rapper friends, some of whom were the best rhymers on the scene. Mark had a studio set up in his basement, and his friends came over and laid down their rhymes over Mark's brilliant mixes. A new art form, encompassing many genres, was taking root.

Soon Dana, Ramsey, and Shakim started spending most of their free time in Mark's basement. Dana loved the vibe of people working together and perfecting beats and rhymes. It wasn't just having fun—it was creative, collaborative, and precise. As she lent her powerful voice for backups, she felt she was part of something bigger than herself.

In the mid-1980s, rapping was still a man's domain, and with the exception of a few lady rappers at the Latin Quarter, rapping just wasn't something that women did. Ramsey, who knew Dana to play football and karate and fire handguns with precision, had no problem seeing Dana as an MC and breaking through those gender barriers. One day, Ramsey handed her the microphone, encouraging her to try a rhyme:

"Come on, Dana, you know you can rock this jam."

He must have read her mind. She'd been composing raps and rhymes in her head for some time, but was hesitant to try them out in front of other people.

Although she knew how they were supposed to sound in her head, her first attempt didn't go well. Nevertheless, Dana still felt that rap was in her DNA, and that it was just a matter of making the connection from what she heard in her head to how she made it sound through a microphone. She recalled her first speech class her junior year. At a speech competition, she completely bungled her rendition of Martin Luther King, Jr.'s "I Have a Dream." Humiliated but not defeated, she began practicing her delivery until it was perfect, and eventually she became an excellent public speaker. Applying the same strategy to rapping, she continued to practice, digging deep inside for the confidence that lay beneath her fears.

The guys, already expert rappers, must have sensed that Dana possessed lyrical genius because they encouraged her efforts, teaching her everything they knew and giving her valuable advice. When she threw down a rap that wasn't "tight," they let her know so that she'd work harder. Sparing her feelings would only lead her to humiliation and failure, and Dana was incredibly grateful for their honesty. She knew she was getting a rare gift in these jamming sessions and walked a fine line between confidence and humility: the confidence to try something just out of reach, and the humility to accept criticism gracefully.

The guys, it seemed, had a dual view of Dana. On the one hand, she was just one of the guys, who could rap, play sports, and "hang tough" in the Latin Quarter. On the other hand, she was an attractive girl who was strong and delicate at the same time. Once again, Dana's unusual upbringing helped her stand head and shoulders above the rest—both physically and mentally.

Those afternoons in Mark's basement were fun for Dana and her friends, but more important, they were constructive. They weren't just goofing off and having fun pretending to be rap stars; they were committed to being the best, knowing that being the best would lead to success and that dreaming would lead only to more daydreams. To be the best, they had to play harder and better than the next person. They had to study the masters. They had to find their own special style, or *flavor*, as they called it.

As they all began to improve their rhymes and find their rapper identities, they built a special bond. The group started calling themselves the Flavor Unit. From the start, they knew that Dana was something special, and they affectionately started calling her the "Princess of the Posse" because she was the only girl in the group. Little did they know that their beloved princess would soon become a revered queen.

It wasn't long before Dana was taking her raps and rhymes to school. She and her girlfriends would hang out in the girls' bathroom between classes and at lunch, beating on trashcans and sinks, and rapping and rhyming with each other. Dana singlehandedly brought rap to the girls of Irvington. She formed Irvington's first girl rap group, Ladies Fresh, and their popularity spread fast. Soon other girl rap groups were cropping up around the school, but instead of feeling threatened by them, Dana befriended them. She created an environment of healthy competition and encouragment, with the girls helping each other get better and refusing to participate in trash talk. It was Dana's nature to be loving, kind, and encouraging. Unlike many male rappers who often had hostile rivalries, she wanted women rappers to stick together.

Rap lyrics, to her dismay, were often **misogynistic** in nature. Embracing an art form that seemed hateful toward women might have seemed counterintuitive, but Dana had a plan, and would soon unleash her own flavor of rap. In the meantime, she encouraged the girls' groups to work with each other, not against each other. Her natural inclination toward diplomacy was yet another clue to her inherent royalty.

Graduation and College

Dana's senior year at Irvington was a whirlwind of friends, music, sports, and studying hard. She'd always loved poetry, but during her senior year, she was introduced to the African American poet Nikki Giovanni. She appreciated Giovanni's ability to express her experience as a black woman through rhyme and rhythm. Dana also continued to hone her own speech skills by frequently engaging in heated and intelligent debates about apartheid in South Africa and racism in America. The poetry of Nikki Giovanni and the colorful and often painful history of black people in America and around the world began to influence the content of her raps. Dana knew she had a voice that commanded attention, and she intended to say something important with that voice.

On the basketball court, she continued to dominate, scoring the winning points during the state finals. Her coach would often put her in charge of team morale, asking her to lead the team in a rap that would put them in a victorious frame of mind. At the boys' basketball games, Ladies Fresh would light up the audience at halftime. It seemed that everything Dana touched turned to gold.

Dana graduated in 1987, just a few months after her seventeenth birthday. Her classmates named her "Most Popular," "Most Comical," "Best Dancer," and "Best All Around" at the senior polls. It was a glorious and exciting day for Dana, being surrounded by so many friends, but nothing meant more to her than having her mother, Winki, and her father watching her from the audience as she received her diploma. The divorce had long since been finalized, but true to their word, Rita and Lance Sr. put their differences aside and worked together for the sake of their children. Even through the divorce, Dana felt a strong sense of family.

DANA A. ELAINE OWENS

Dana was a gifted athlete and popular with her classmates. She remembers her high school days fondly.

With her good grades and ambition, it was no question for Dana that her next step would be heading off to college. She had entertained different dream occupations her whole life, including marine biologist, lawyer, and newscaster. Hoping for the best of both worlds she enrolled at the Borough of Manhattan Community College, majoring in broadcast journalism, while still living with her mom and brother in Newark. They had recently moved to an apartment at the corner of Halstead and Elmwood Avenues, which sat above the Modern Era Barbershop. Manhattan seemed to be the ticket to her dreams, but home was always in New Jersey. She had the best of both worlds and couldn't be happier.

Ramsey, however, had bigger plans for Dana. Although not a rapper himself, he was a genius at recognizing talent and bringing out the best in artists. While the individual members of the Flavor Unit focused on being the best rappers, Ramsey focused on opportunities. He had a vision of the group becoming not just entertainers but shrewd business people who would dominate the hip-hop music industry and give local people jobs. He didn't dream of making it big and moving away. He dreamt of returning Newark to its former glory. Just as her parents used to drive through nice neighborhoods saying they'd live there someday, Ramsey drove through dilapidated neighborhoods saying, "We'll fix this up someday."

Under his tutelage, one by one, members of the Flavor Unit started scoring recording contracts with **music labels**. Although Dana loved rapping, she didn't think the world would accept her flavor of hip-hop. Ramsey felt otherwise and encouraged her to cut a **demo**, a recording that artists distribute to producers in hopes of getting a recording contract. They practiced in Mark's basement until she had the perfect sound, then took that sound to a recording studio. Ramsey paid for the recording studio out of his own pocket, risking eviction and bankruptcy. Dana knew that time was money, and she was focused and poised when she entered the recording booth, yet another sign that she was a born pro.

Unfortunately, Ramsey was not able to get record producers interested in a female rapper, and the demo opened no doors. Dana felt terrible that Ramsey had spent his time and money for nothing, but Ramsey felt he had let her down. Nevertheless, he wouldn't let Dana quit. He knew she had something special, and that he had to get her music in front of the right people.

What Dana saw as good, Mark and Ramsey saw as spectacular. The next day, Mark put that demo tape in the hands of his DJ friend Fab Five Freddy, who had recently started hosting a hit show on MTV called *Yo! MTV Raps*. Not long after, Dana was sitting in her kitchen, switching between radio stations when she heard a familiar beat. Her heart stopped. Was she dreaming? No, she was awake, and she was listening to her own voice on the radio belting out "Princess of the Posse." Elated, she ran from room to room opening windows and shouting down to the streets,

"My record is on the radio!"

By this time, the various members of the Flavor Unit had put New Jersey on the map of hip-hop. Before that, no one wanted to admit they were from Jersey, but true to Ramsey's dreams, Jersey was quickly becoming Rap Central.

The hosts of *Yo! MTV Raps*, Dr. Dre (left), Fab 5 Freddy (center), and Ed Lover (right) helped bring rap to a wider audience in the late 1980s.

A Recording Contract

One day after hearing her song on the radio, Dana came in from the basketball court and the phone rang. On the line was a woman named Monica Lynch, who was vice president of artist development at Tommy Boy Records, and she wanted to meet with Dana to discuss a recording contract. Dana's head was spinning. She was barely eighteen and still living at home, but a major label wanted to sign her. The first thing she did was burst into Winki's room to tell him the good news: She was getting a record deal!

Always one to count her blessings and remember those who helped her in life, she thought about all the people who got her to this moment. There was her mother, who found a way to give her music lessons even when they were struggling, and who trusted her when she went to the Latin Quarter, where she was immersed in the hip-hop culture. There was her father, who taught her that she could be anything she wanted to be and how to be a strong woman in a man's world. There was Winki, who was with her every step of the way and who gave her her first job, which enabled to her buy the music that helped influence her. There was Irvington High School and its dedicated English teachers, who showed her the beauty of poetry and the written word. There were her coach and teammates, who helped her understand the importance of discipline and practice. There was Shakim, who thought so highly of her that he cleaned up his act just to spend time with her. There was Ramsey, who lived on mayonnaise sandwiches for months so that he could pay for Dana's demo tape. There was Mark the 45 King and all the members of the Flavor Unit, who took her art seriously and demanded the best from her.

Dana relished this feeling, realizing that everything she had done in her life led her to this moment. She was a poor girl from a broken family in a broken city, and yet she continually found herself surrounded by people who encouraged her to rise above her surroundings. She vowed there and then that she would make good on her promise to make her friends and family proud, and that she would someday pay them all back.

CHAPTER FIVE

A Queen Is Born

While Dana was ecstatic to be invited to sign a contract with Tommy Boy Records, she still wasn't free and clear on the road to fame and wealth. Record labels are notorious for sometimes cheating artists out of their hard-earned money. Executives often come from a business background and have been carefully mentored on how to get the most from artists with the least amount of investment. Contracts are usually written to benefit the label, not the artists, and many artists wind up penniless despite churning out hit records.

Black artists in particular have suffered at the hands of greedy label executives. Artists such as Jimi Hendrix and the Supremes, who sold millions of records, were

notoriously abused and duped by their labels. Rita
didn't want her daughter to suffer at the hands of these
professional crooks who thought nothing of taking
advantage of children.

Dana was eighteen and not technically a child
anymore, but she was still naïve about business dealings,
so Rita insisted that they hire a lawyer to help her
through the negotiation process. Mark, Ramsey, and her
friends from the Flavor Unit also offered her advice on
dealing with executives. She might have been young and
naïve, but she wasn't about to let the record company
think they could take advantage of her.

The Name

When it came time to sign the contracts, her lawyer
asked what her "p.k.a."—"professionally known as"—
name would be. Dana had dreamed about this day
since the early days of jamming with the Flavor Unit.
She knew she wanted "Latifah" to be part of her stage
persona. It was the identity she created when she was
just eight years old, and that identity helped her grow
into the talented, strong young woman she was now. But
"Latifah" sounded too plain. A rap superstar needed a
big name. She thought of MC Latifah, but all the male
rappers used MC, and she wanted to stand out and make
a statement. She considered "Princess Latifah," since
that's what her Flavor Unit brothers liked to call her, but
Princess evoked images of a spoiled and sheltered girl,

and that hardly described how Dana was raised.

When she thought of power, she kept seeing images of the African queens in the books her mother gave her as a child. These women were not only beautiful, they were also fierce. They were regal in a way that transcended material wealth. She loved the way they held their heads high and the look of determination in their eyes.

Self-confidence was a major theme in rap music, but would calling herself "Queen" be taking confidence to the realm of arrogance? To Dana, "queen" represented a way of conducting oneself and how one thinks of oneself. A queen commands respect not because of her title but because of her accomplishments. The African queens she admired as a child were her ancestors, and she chose that day to pay homage to them by behaving like a queen and encouraging women to find their inner queen. With this in mind, Queen Latifah was born.

When she told her mother about her newly chosen name, she rolled her eyes as if Dana were out of her mind. "How are you going to call yourself 'Queen'?" she asked. Dana was undaunted. Rap was her calling, Queen Latifah was her name, and hip-hop would be her kingdom. She was about to unleash her royal badness upon the world.

The Image

Image is an important part of performing. A well-crafted image is all part of an artist's branding and is an extension of his or her artistic expression. The handful of female rap stars on the scene had made a splash with their sexuality, taking full advantage of the adage "Sex sells." Dana was uncomfortable with that image. At five feet ten inches, she had an athletic build. All of her life, she worried that she was too big and not feminine enough for society's idea of beauty. It was time for Queen Latifah to redefine beauty to include all shapes, sizes, and shades of women. Femininity was about to have a new flavor.

Queen Latifah makes power look beautiful.

The women who inspired her strength and lyrics would also inspire her image, and just like her name and her attitude, she wanted her clothing to reflect African royalty. She went to a local store that carried traditional African fabrics, looked through her old history books, and asked the seamstress to create some outfits for her, complete with African jewelry and hats. Dana knew that individuality was the key to distinguishing herself among many talented artists, and with her new image, no one would ever confuse her for another female rapper. There could be only one queen.

The Message

Rap music proved to be more than a passing fad. Unfortunately, the general public challenged the notion that rap was singing, or even an art form. Despite being a vehicle for change, rap's image was tarnished by many groups who glorified murder, drugs, and rape. By the time Queen Latifah came on the scene, mainstream media regarded rappers as dangerous thugs who inspired listeners to perpetrate more violence.

Queen Latifah had a broader vision of rap. To her and many other African Americans, rap was an urban form of poetry, and it took incredible skill and precision to create rhymes and rhythms to the backdrop of music. She maintained that rap was not only a means for enter-tainment but also a legitimate art form for people like her to voice their frustrations with society. Like many other

African Americans, she thought it was time for America to hear its history from another point of view.

She could not, however, support the themes of glorifying violence and objectifying women that were so prevalent in rap music. Even more perplexing to Dana were the women who supported these themes in rap music. Either they didn't bother listening to lyrics or they felt they had to go along with the abuse in order to be accepted. Just as she witnessed her father reprimand a man who was beating a woman on the street, she knew it was her turn to take a stand.

Taking her music in this direction was a huge risk, which she carefully weighed. Men dominated the rap scene, and women ironically were known to distance themselves from anyone who challenged them for fear that the very men who oppressed them would not like them. She thought of all the lessons her mother taught her about treating yourself with dignity, and realized that these women may not have had such a presence in their lives. No one had taught them how to be strong. Hip-hop was not just a genre to Dana. She saw it as a movement, an opportunity for people like her to raise their voices and to inspire others. She hoped to be an influence of strength and grace to girls and women who were sorely lacking in role models.

Touring and Tribulations

When the record deal came, Dana had to make some

hard choices about her life and the direction in which it was headed. College was not just an option to Dana; it was an obligation. All the years of watching her mother put herself through school while working and raising children inspired Dana, and besides that, she loved learning. However, with record deals come huge responsibilities to make music, practice, record, go on interviews, and tour the world. With a heavy heart, she broke the news to her mother: She was leaving college, at least temporarily.

At first, Rita was stunned and disturbed. Giving up a college education to try to be a rap star? The idea must have seemed not only absurd but also scary—but again, she saw the look in Dana's eyes and knew this was not a passing fancy. This was a calling. Within months of being signed, Dana's record company arranged tours to Germany and Japan, places she had read about her entire life but never imagined seeing in person. Knowing that experience is often the best education, Rita gave Dana her blessing to embark on this new journey. Yet again, she knew she had to trust Dana to navigate her life with sound decisions and ceaseless courage.

Touring proved to be more than a lesson in geography; it was also an education in negotiating. Although the label supported her in many ways, Dana was left to fend for herself when it came to concert **promoters**. Just a teenager and new to the industry, many promoters assumed she was weak and naïve and tried to take advantage of her. It was commonplace for a promoter to promise one amount, and then attempt to offer only half of that at the conclusion of a gig. Tired of arguing and fighting for what was rightfully hers, she turned to her friend Shakim. One night at a concert, as usual, a promoter was taking far more than his share, so she sent Shakim to deal with him. Within minutes, he returned, cash in hand. Was this shrewd and confident businessman the same boy whom just a few years earlier she had to convince to stay in school?

Dana asked Shakim to handle the promoters, and she turned her focus on giving her best performances. Shakim already had a full-time job, but when Dana asked him to be her business manager, he gladly obliged. He is still her manager to this day. She couldn't help but count her blessings yet again. She'd be on the road, but she'd be taking part of Jersey with her in the form of her longtime friend. Dana would never be one to forget how she got where she was and who helped her get there. She knew in her heart that no matter where Queen Latifah went, she would always be "Dana from around the way" to those who knew and loved her.

Queen Latifah's career started moving at an exciting pace. Her songs, which openly criticized the pervasive themes of misogyny in rap music, were a sensation. After releasing a few successful singles, Tommy Boy released her first album, *All Hail the Queen*, in 1989. It was a bestseller that was also met with positive reviews from music critics. Critic Alex Henderson called her rapping skills "top notch" and her songs "hard-hitting," while critic Robert Christgrau commended her underlying allegiance to her ancestors: "It's a relief to hear a woman grab onto the mother-worship that's an unhonored subtext of male rap Afrocentrism—the feminist instincts."

Her compelling video for the single "Ladies First," in which she invited other female rappers to appear and join in **solidarity**, caught the curious attention of many critics, producers, and executives. Queen Latifah proved herself to be not only a lyrical genius and powerhouse performer but also a visual artist who commanded brilliant use of metaphor.

All Hail the Queen went on to sell over a million copies and climbed to number six on *Billboard's* hip-hop charts. More importantly, the album earned Queen Latifah a Grammy nomination, the first woman in her category to do so. Critics and audiences alike praised Queen Latifah for the bravery, self-respect, and social-consciousness her lyrics championed. Many critics credited her with making rap music a legitimate art form that transcended race and gender lines

Shakim was still managing Queen Latifah's skyrocketing career, and they considered themselves business partners. Record sales were through the roof, and with that came proceeds from record sales, tours, merchandise, and appearances. At just nineteen years old, they were suddenly thrust into a world of shrewd

and often crooked business associates. After they both
admittedly blew some of their proceeds on foolish
purchases, such as expensive yet gaudy jewelry and a gold
tooth that Dana still laughs about today, they agreed
that they should hire a professional to look after their
finances. It was important to both of them to send money
to both their families, put some away for the future, and
enjoy some of their wealth. Hiring an accountant from
a prestigious Manhattan accounting firm was the next
logical step, and they felt instant relief knowing they were
being wise with their money.

Dana loved the financial freedom that her stardom brought, but
she learned the hard way that managing finances is more difficult
than it seems.

A few years later, they received devastating news from the professional they hired to manage their accounts: they were nearly broke. For the second time in her life, Dana knew what it was like to lose everything. They were justifiably angry, but picked up the pieces and started over.

Hollywood Calling

By 1991 Queen Latifah was tearing up the airways and riding high on the wave of success. She couldn't imagine life being better than this—doing what she loved, challenging societal conventions, and making her family, her race, and her gender proud. She was aware of the positive impact she was having in the music world, but Hollywood was keeping a close eye on her, too.

Spike Lee was one of the hottest Hollywood directors by the early 1990s, fresh off the success of his critically acclaimed film *Do the Right Thing*. When he called Queen Latifah to offer her a role in his upcoming film *Jungle Fever*, starring Wesley Snipes, she had to pinch herself. She had harbored dreams of being an actress since she was a little girl, when her mother took her to movies, plays, and musicals, and now she was about to make her Hollywood debut.

Although *Jungle Fever* didn't receive the critical praise that *Do the Right Thing* did, Queen Latifah caught the eye of many Hollywood critics for her role as an outspoken cafe waitress. Roles in the films *House Party 2* and *Juice* soon followed, and many wondered if the queen of rap would give up her throne for the silver screen. Little did they know she was already hard at work on her follow-up album, *Nature of a Sistah*.

Queen Latifah proudly dons her royal threads.

Nature of a Sistah

Released in 1992, *Nature of a Sistah* was a bit of a departure from her debut album, as she explored the many styles of music she loved as a youngster. Still a rap album at its core, she introduced a new sound with her blend of reggae, R & B (rhythm and blues), and funk undertones. As for her lyrics, Queen Latifah still had a lot on her mind, and the revolution she helped launch needed a new anthem.

While Tommy Boy tolerated her artistic ambitions for her first album, they tried to reign in her energy and creative license for her second album, fearful that she would lose the delicate balance she struck with mainstream audiences on her first album. The queen, however, felt she should be sole commander of her new work, and as a result her relationship with the label was strained.

To her delight, audiences and critics loved her latest effort, and she was nominated with yet another Grammy, this time taking home the trophy for Best Solo Rap Performance with her song "Fly Girl." When record sales failed to surpass *All Hail the Queen*, Tommy Boy terminated the contract, proving they were more interested in financial gain than in critical success.

Barely in her twenties, Queen Latifah had toured the world, made and lost a fortune, won a Grammy, landed a choice role in a Hollywood movie, and had just lost a major recording contract. In tumultuous times like these, she reached out to her mother, brother, and the gang from New Jersey. Dana had no idea that in just a few short months, tragedy would strike again. However, this time, she would never completely recover.

CHAPTER SIX

Picking Up the Pieces

Stardom comes with many strings attached. Recording, filming, and touring for nearly two solid years left Dana feeling depleted and detached. After her recording contract fell through with Tommy Boy, she realized it was a good time to get back to Jersey and spend time with the friends and family who sustained her. Many of her friends from Jersey's Rap Central, who were now successful rap stars, had bought homes back in their hometown, and Dana also wanted to keep her connection to home alive.

Life had been good to the Owens while Dana was on tour. Rita had been honored by the governor as a top educator in New Jersey, and Winki had just been inducted into the Newark police force and was engaged to be married. In the previous two years, she'd seen her family every chance she could, but spent most of her time driving from one person's apartment to the next. To minimize the time wasted driving between houses, Dana solved the problem by buying a house that she, her mother, and brother could all live in together.

Just like they did when they were younger, they drove around Newark neighborhoods, but this time, they were not just dreaming—they were buying! They chose a house that was still being built in Wayne, in an upscale suburban neighborhood. It had a huge backyard surrounded by woods, plenty of skylights, and a modern architectural style. It was big enough for each of them to have bedrooms and living space on separate floors, as well as plenty of shared spaces, such as the kitchen and dining room, where they looked forward to spending time together. With Dana's rap friends and Winki's police friends, they knew their house would always be full of love and good times.

They giddily discussed how they would decorate their respective floors and shared spaces. Dana had already picked out a beautiful burl wood bedroom suite for Rita that she had seen in Los Angeles, as well as a leather bedroom suite for Winki, and she couldn't wait to surprise them. They even had a Jacuzzi installed in the backyard. This house was going to be beyond their wildest childhood dreams! Winki knew a little about carpentry, and he and Dana loved to jump on their motorcycles and ride into Chinatown in Manhattan to check out the specialty plumbing and lighting stores. Every detail about their family's dream home was going to be special.

Motorcycles were a new love for Dana and Winki. Shakim had turned Dana on to the glory of open roads. After one ride, Dana knew it was something Winki would love, too. For his twenty-fourth birthday, she surprised him with a brand-new bike, a Kawasaki Ninja ZX7. Riding with Winki on the open roads made her feel like they did when they were kids—young, carefree, and excited about life. Winki had always helped Dana embrace adventure, and buying him the motorcycle was her way of thanking him for being that driving force in her life. They were now two successful young adults in promising careers, surrounded by loved ones. They'd come a long way since their days in the projects. They both had the world by the tail, and they loved every second of life.

Tragedy Strikes

It was a gorgeous sunny day in Newark, and Dana was hanging with some of her Rao Central friends. Most of them were stars in their own right, but like Dana, they never forgot where they got their start. They had just spent the day helping their buddy Latee move into a new house and were talking about the good old days, when Dana received an emergency page (this was before cell phones) from Ramsey. Winki had been in a motorcycle accident.

Shakim drove Dana to the hospital, when an ominous cloud seemed to swallow the whole sky. As rain pelted the windshield, an eerie feeling washed over Dana. She suddenly felt detached, as if floating without an anchor. Dana explains the horrible feeling that came over her as thus, "I wasn't prepared, but I already knew. Winki and I had this connection—a bond… We always knew what the other was thinking. It was the type of spiritual kinship that only the tightest of siblings can share. But something told me our tie had been severed." Just then a wrecking truck passed them, towing a mangled motorcycle that was the same make, model, and color as Winki's.

When she arrived at the emergency room, Winki's friends were already there, and some of them nearly broke down when they saw her. She was led to the family waiting room, where her mother took her in her arms. Rita had always had been brave for her children, and Dana knew it must be serious because she was inexplicably calm. At that point Dana went from praying to God to begging Him not to take her brother, her rock, her best friend. When a doctor finally emerged from the operating room, Dana knew immediately it was bad news: The doctors could not save him. Winki had died.

In a state of shock, Dana walked outside, trying to catch her breath, but instead sobbed uncontrollably. Angry and confused, she screamed at passing cars and ambulances, but nothing could relieve the pressure of her grief.

Her mother remained steadfast for Dana, being the strong one whenever they were together, so Dana could cry freely. Her father began to spend time with Rita and Dana, but he was suffering in a different way. He was suddenly aware of how much of Winki's life he missed when he and Rita were separated. Realizing he could never get that time back, he openly broke down in front of his daughter and ex-wife. Dana would often try to make deals with God—pleading with Him to take away everything else in her life but to give her Winki. Moments like these would set her back in her grief, and she remained in a state of shock and denial for months. As Dana said,

> *"Every morning and every evening, grief pounded at my skull, tearing through my heart. Losing Winki was like losing half myself. I was numb and empty."*

Immediately following Winki's death, she spent most of her time with her friend and former teammate, Tammy. When Dana wanted to lash out at God and denounce her faith, Tammy reeled her back. Having lost her own mother three years prior, Tammy became a source of comfort and strength for Dana. Tammy helped her find her faith again, but internally, Dana suffered for years and looked for ways to numb the pain.

Denial, Depression, and Drug Dependency

Growing up in a city like Newark, Dana had been exposed to various vices her entire childhood, but that was nothing compared to what was readily available to her in the entertainment industry. Overall, she had been a good kid growing up. She had her unauthorized forays into the city and other things she experimented with, but between her good sense and solid upbringing, she always managed to stay in control of her actions. She never wanted to find herself trapped in the inner city poverty cycle, which always seemed to stem from drugs and promiscuous sex.

Despite her best intentions, after Winki died, Dana began to feel hopeless and spiraled into a depression, fueled with alcohol and controlled substances. "I was numb. Angry. Guilty. I had every kind of negative emotion. I blamed God. I blamed myself," she said. "Prayer, as much as I am ashamed to admit it, was not enough to keep me straight... My feelings were blunted, and I was blunted—literally... Every morning before I opened my eyes, I would be crying." She spent hours on the basketball court pounding anger into the pavement, but for the first time in her life, playing hoops brought her no relief.

Just as she was falling apart on the inside, her career was escalating beyond her wildest dreams. She and Shakim had recently launched their own production company, Flavor Unit Entertainment, and were making plans to launch a new record label. She had lost her recording contract with Tommy Boy, but another label called Motown had recently signed her, and she had been looking forward to writing songs for her third album. Hollywood also wanted her. Fox Television was about to air a new sitcom called *Living Single*, and the leading role had been written specifically for Queen Latifah.

Success, Grief, and Gratitude

Everyone agreed that Dana should embrace these opportunities and attempt to move on with her life. Moving to sunny Los Angeles seemed like a good start. *Living Single* was a smash hit, receiving not only record viewership and critical praise, but accolades for being the first Hollywood depiction of young black women as ambitious professionals and witty comedians. Many people looked to the cast of *Living Single*, which included Queen Latifah, the grown-up child star Kim Fields, Kim Coles, Erika Alexander, John Henton, and Terrence T.C. Carson, as role models for success. Queen Latifah penned and sang the theme song, which became yet another anthem for black American women.

Dana loved being on the show and felt a personal connection to her character, Khadija James. The Queen Latifah image was a sort of street-smart stage presence she needed to command huge stadiums, but on the small screen, she loved to be able to show her tender, nurturing side, and Khadija fit that bill perfectly. In many episodes, Khadija can be seen wearing a gold necklace with a key dangling from it. Dana had the necklace made from Winki's motorcycle key and kept it around her neck for years as a way to keep him close.

The show continued to soar in success for the next five years. Despite letters pouring in from fans, positive reviews, and major corporate sponsorship, Fox inexplicably cancelled the series in 1998. The cast was heartbroken. The show wasn't just their ticket to success, it was a meaningful contribution to society and particularly to black culture. Having the plug pulled felt like a betrayal, and audiences were outraged.

After her brother Winki's accident, Queen Latifah made a necklace from his motorcycle key so that she could always keep him close.

As if starring on a hit television show weren't enough to keep her busy, Dana found time to write and record songs for her next albums. Using the grief and anger she felt at losing Winki and the love she felt from friends and family during this time of loss, she wrote what many call her best work. Her phenomenal third album, *Black Reign*, released at the end of 1993, was a sensation the second it hit the airways, and it became her best-selling album to date. This deeply personal album was the first album by a female rap singer to reach the music business level **certified gold**, selling over a million copies.

Her call-to-arms song "U.N.I.T.Y." garnered attention far and wide for its thought-provoking lyrics, which denounced the usage of derogatory terms for women in rap music. The anthem earned her another Grammy Award. The final track, "Winki's Theme," was Dana's tribute to her brother. She wrote it in the bedroom of the New Jersey home she never got to share with him, going into something of a trance as she dug deep for the lyrics. Writing it helped her work through a lot of the pain that drugs and alcohol could never alleviate, and it gave her a sense of Winki's immortality.

With a gold record and hit TV series, Dana showed no signs of slowing down. She went on to make more Hollywood films, such as the critically acclaimed but somewhat controversial 1996 film *Set It Off*. Her portrayal of Cleo earned her the American Black Film Festival Award for Best Actress, as well as nominations

Queen Latifah gives her audiences a moving performance no matter the genre of music.

for the Independent Spirit Awards and the **National Association for the Advancement of Colored People (NAACP)** Image Awards. Despite the awards, she faced some criticism. People wondered why, after working so hard to be a positive role model, she would portray a negative character. Others felt that her portrayal of the character was deeply complex and compelling and that African Americans should be encouraged to take on such serious roles.

Talk Show 1.0

After *Living Single* was cancelled, Queen Latifah was approached to host a talk show. At first she was thrilled, hoping to use her influence as a way to showcase emerging talents in the hip-hop world and to discuss important topics that mattered to her. It also presented her with the chance to live out her college dreams of becoming a newscaster. Unfortunately, the producers of the show had other ideas and wanted the show to be modeled after the *Jerry Springer Show*, which was notorious for its risqué themes and frequent on-air brawls between guests. Despite being the queen of hip-hop, Dana was still tender at heart, and the dark themes of the daily shows began to weigh on her. The show lasted two seasons, and when it was cancelled, Dana felt relieved that she could go on to do things that mattered to her.

The School of Hard Knocks

Flavor Unit Entertainment, the production company she founded with Shakim, which was once full of promise, was in trouble. They'd just launched a record label and had signed many artists, including LL Cool J, Outkast, and Naughty by Nature. The operations, however, grew more quickly than their business. In their desire to be generous with friends and family, they gave them all high-paying jobs. However, many of their friends and family members were not cut out for the work of managing a major record label. Soon, more money was flowing out than flowing in, and Dana and Shakim received a crushing blow from their accountant: they were again broke. This was the second time in their relatively short career that they had won and lost a fortune, and from that day forward they vowed to educate themselves to ensure it would never happen again.

Once again, they started from scratch. They dropped all but their most successful artists and were forced to lay off their friends and family, keeping only a handful of essential employees. It was a hard decision, but they realized they were partially to blame for handing out jobs and turning a blind eye to some questionable work ethics.

In addition to letting her guard down about her business, Dana had unfortunately also let her guard down in other areas of her life. For a few years, she was doing battle with inner demons. In 1995, she was the victim of a carjacking in Harlem, during which a close friend was shot in the stomach. The incident left her frazzled and paranoid, and she turned to marijuana again to ease her jitters. She also began carrying a handgun to protect herself. Unfortunately, during a routine traffic stop, a police officer found her in possession of marijuana and a concealed weapon and arrested her. A few years later, she was arrested for driving under the influence and received three years' probation. Part of her sentencing included drug and alcohol counseling. She began seeing a therapist at the advice of her friend, actress Jada Pinkett Smith, and through intense sessions she was able to work through some repressed traumas.

Her crown might have been tarnished, but a true queen always picks herself up and stands tall. She began to talk openly about her demons and her business failures as a means to help her understand her actions and in the hope that others could learn from her mistakes. As always, Dana looked for the silver lining. The next decade would bring Queen Latifah a level of success she wouldn't have dreamed of in a million years.

NEW!

INSPIRED BY QUEEN LATIFAH, DESIGNED FOR WOMEN OF COLO

THE COVERGIRL QUEEN COLLECTION

A rich spectrum of advanced cosmetics — new formulas, colors
and foundations — designed to match, not mask, your beautiful sk

BECAUSE EVERY WOMAN IS A QUEEN.

Queen Latifah wears Golden Honey Powder Foundation; LionQueen
Eyeshadow Quads; Black Onyx Eyeliner; and Diamond Drop Lip Gloss.

visit covergirl.com/queen or call 1-800 4COVER4
for store locations and for more information

COVERGIRL® QUEEN
COLLECTIO

NEW YORK · CHICAGO · LOS ANGELES · ATLANTA · WASHINGTON, DC · BALTIMORE · PHILADELPHIA · DETROIT · HOUSTON · DALLAS · MIAMI
RALEIGH-DURHAM · MEMPHIS · NORFOLK · CLEVELAND · NEW ORLEANS · ST. LOUIS · SACRAMENTO

CHAPTER SEVEN

The Queen of Reinvention

From navigating the transition from college student to hip-hop artist, to becoming a well-regarded actress, to choosing her own, regal name, Queen Latifah has truly demonstrated an ability to choose exactly who it is she wants to be. Never one to rest on her laurels, she constantly sought new opportunities in every facet of show business. By the year 2000, she had a long list of credentials: Grammy-winning singer, television star, Hollywood actress, movie producer, record label owner, and bestselling author. She had overcome addictions, faced her demons, and was still considered a top role model for girls.

Redefining Beauty

The saying "Beauty is in the eye of the beholder" is often used to remind people that beauty should not be defined by a certain standard or confined by certain ideals. Fashion magazines, Hollywood movies, and the music industry, however, are notorious for reinforcing unattainable beauty standards. For many women, it's not enough to have talent—they feel they must also be stunningly beautiful. Growing up, Dana was like most girls and loved to pore over magazines and admire fashions, hairstyles, and makeup trends. The problem was that, like most girls, what she saw staring back on those glossy pages never resembled what she saw in the mirror. Even in magazines geared toward an African American audience, such as *Ebony* and *Jet*, she saw mainly light-skinned women who were skin and bones.

Queen Latifah helped redefine beauty with her CoverGirl cosmetic line.

It seemed that girls like Dana were being told that they could be beautiful only if they strongly resembled skinny white women. When Dana took on the persona of Queen Latifah, she aspired to look like her powerful African queen ancestors, and her fans went wild for her look. In her own way, she redefined beauty for herself, and in doing so, she slowly started to see her physical beauty. Knowing that her opinion of herself mattered more than anyone else's, she began to love everything about her face, skin, and body. Perhaps it was this expression of inner self-love that transformed her visage because all of a sudden, everyone seemed to be noticing not only her talent but also her beauty.

When the makeup company CoverGirl offered her an endorsement deal and the chance to design her own cosmetic line, Queen Latifah couldn't believe it. Not only was she dark-skinned, she was also plus sized, two traits that did not conform to the mainstream idea of beauty.

"I always felt beautiful in my own way… I believed it would completely change the lives of millions of girls, and that gave me a thrill…It was going to expand the idea of beauty in a way that was long overdue. Young black, Latina, Indian, and Asian girls would see it."

Modeling for fashion shoots was a joy for her. She knew that girls would no longer look at magazines and movies and feel unworthy because they didn't look a certain way.

A Nod from Oscar

In the nineties she was queen of the music scene, but by the early 2000s, it was clear that Queen Latifah was about to reign over the silver screen. Starring with top performers such as Denzel Washington, Angelina Jolie, Danny DeVito, Ice Cube, Holly Hunter, Sharon Stone, and Dustin Hoffman helped her realize that she had to take her acting career more seriously. Hiring an acting coach, she put the word out that she was looking for diverse roles. Offers soon came knocking. At one point it seemed that Queen Latifah barely had to lift a finger to get a role in an upcoming film.

In 2002, however, the queen had to fight for the role of a lifetime. The Broadway smash musical *Chicago* was going to be adapted to a film version, and Dana had her eye on the role of Mama Morton. Auditioning three times, she finally beat out contenders Bette Midler, Rosie O'Donnell, and Kathy Bates for the juicy role. Dana modeled the character after her grandmother, channeling her unstoppable energy and razor-sharp wit.

Chicago was one the most anticipated films of 2002 and starred Hollywood's hottest actors, including Richard Gere, Renee Zellwegger, Catherine Zeta-Jones, and

John C. Reilly. What's more, the film enabled Queen Latifah to showcase all her talents: acting, singing, and dancing. All of the musicals her mother took her to as a child culminated in this tremendous opportunity, and Queen Latifah's Mama Morton took audiences by storm.

The Academy of Motion Pictures and Sciences was also impressed with Queen Latifah's performance and nominated her for an Oscar in the category of Best Supporting Actress. Queen Latifah was the first rap star to ever receive the honor of an Oscar nomination. Although Catherine Zeta-Jones ultimately took home the trophy, Queen Latifah was now considered a certified cinematic gold mine. Audiences could not get enough of her, and she continued to light up the screen in role after role.

Starring in the movie *Last Holiday* helped Dana remember to enjoy the good things in life.

Although some dismissed it as romantic comedy (RomCom) fluff piece, one of Dana's favorite roles was Georgia Byrd in the 2006 film *Last Holiday*. Dana starred alongside LL Cool J. On the surface, the movie was lighthearted, but to Dana, it was a much-needed reminder to herself to enjoy every day. Her life had been a whirlwind of love, excitement, tragedy, loss, and success, and the film reminded her to take time to do the things she loved most.

Another life-changing role for Dana was in the 2007 film *Life Support*. A much more serious film, Dana portrayed real-life **AIDS** activist Ana Willis. The film, written and directed by Willis's brother—writer, columnist, and filmmaker Nelson George—was the true story of Ana, who had contracted the AIDS virus from her husband when they were both injecting drugs. Although she overcame her addiction to drugs, she lost custody of her oldest daughter and was fighting to win her back, while leading a grass roots crusade to educate the public on how to stop the spread of the epidemic.

Dana's work on the film put her in touch with actual survivors of the virus, which she described as a humbling and inspiring experience. Like *Last Holiday*, it reminded her once again that every minute on this earth is precious. The film premiered to praise at the 2007 Sundance Film Festival and aired on HBO the following month. For her riveting performance, she was nominated for an Emmy Award for Outstanding Lead Actress in a Miniseries or

Movie, and she won the Golden Globe and the Screen
Actors Guild Award for Best Performance by an Actress
in a Miniseries or Television Movie.

Let the Music Play

Although she slowed down the music side of her career
while her acting was taking off, Dana still managed
to release a few more albums. Her 1998 *Order in the
Court* featured fewer rap songs than her previous two
albums and didn't make much of an impact on the music
world. Some complained that she'd given up rap and
had sold out. Although she didn't relish the criticism, it
was important for her to explore all types of music. She
hoped her fans would follow her, but if they didn't, that
was their choice.

In 2004, she released *The Dana Owens Album,* a
tribute to the jazz, blues, and soul classics that made her
want to become a singer in the first place. Unlike her
other albums, this one contained no raps and showcased
her smooth-as-honey vocals. Releasing such an album
was a risk, but it paid off. It became an instant best seller,
selling over a million copies and tantalizing audiences
and critics alike. Queen Latifah once again proved to
have as many facets as a diamond.

Her sixth studio album, *Trav'lin' Light*, similarly
featured all singing and no rapping, and it was nominated
for the 2008 Best Traditional Vocal album. Her favorite
song on that album was a cover of Phoebe Snow's

"Poetry Man," which was one of her mother's favorite songs of all time. Getting the stamp of approval from Rita for that song was better than any Grammy Award.

In 2009, she released *Persona*. Much fanfare surrounded the album, in which she would hearken back to her hip-hop roots. A labor of love, it featured collaborations from many of Queen Latifah's contemporaries, including Missy Elliot, Cool & Dre, Marsha Ambrosius, Busta Rhymes, and Mary J. Blige. It debuted at number 25 on the *Billboard 200*.

An Enduring Star

In 2006, Queen Latifah was awarded a star on the Hollywood Walk of Fame, the first given to a hip-hop artist. She has said that she will never forget that day as long as she lives. Flanked by her mother and father and surrounded by friends, she remembered when she was seventeen and saw the Walk of Fame for the first time:

> *"I knew the only way to get kind of recognition was to accomplish a lot. So for me to have come from I'm from, a regular girl from Newark, New Jersey, it was confirmation that yes, you can do anything."*

On January 4, 2006, when she was presented her star, she wasn't Queen Latifah. She was Dana Owens, a girl from Newark. She hoped that her star might bring inspiration to other girls who, like her, were brought up on the mean streets of an inner city and who didn't fit the traditional model of beauty. She wanted girls to look at her star and say to themselves, "If she can do it, I can do it!" Best of all was the location of her star: right next to Michael Jackson's, one of her many childhood heroes.

In 2010, Dana authored a best-selling book, *Put on Your Crown: Life-Changing Moments on the Path to Queendom*. Like her first book, *Ladies First: Revelations of a Strong Woman*, released over ten years earlier, it was part autobiography and part manifesto for successful living. In writing it she shared the following:

> *"There seems to be an epidemic of lousy self-esteem in this country, especially among young women, and this concerns me deeply. We ladies have stopped putting ourselves first, and I wanted to share something with you that would help you feel empowered and make you recognize the individual and innate beauty that is you."*

As of 2014, Dana has appeared in over forty-one films. Some of her favorites include *Hairspray*, *The Secret Life of Bees*, and *Make a Joyful Noise*, as well as the many animated films for which she did voice-over work. In 2012, she starred in the Lifetime television remake of

Queen Latifah hopes her Hollywood star will inspire other young ladies to become confident and successful women.

Steel Magnolias, alongside Alfre Woodard and Phylicia Rashad. The film drew over 6.5 million viewers, ranking it as the third most watched telecast in the network's history.

The year 2013 marked her return as talk show host. Fourteen years had passed since her first talk show was canceled, and many wondered if she had lost her mind for trying it again. When Sony Pictures approached her about the show, she was intrigued—but insisted that this time, she would run the show, both as a host and

> ### "Reverend" Queen Latifah "Presiding" at the 2014 Grammys
>
> The 2014 Grammys were one of the most publicized awards shows of all time. With rap duo Macklemore & Ryan Lewis (featuring Mary Lambert) singing their hit song "Same Love," a ballad about equality, Queen Latifah officiated over thirty-three marriages of straight, gay, and interracial couples. In the wake of widespread congressional bills banning same sex marriage in the previous weeks, the event inspired a standing ovation, as well as an outpouring of emotions, including the shedding of tears by country superstar Keith Urban. "I look forward to the day when presiding over a historic wedding ceremony like this is the norm," Queen Latifah told the *Los Angeles Times* in an interview the following day. Hip-hop has long been an incubator for social change, and after the ceremony, Queen Latifah stated, "I hope this is inspiration to all the rappers out there and hip-hop artists out there that they can continue to tackle any subjects you want." Although not an ordained minister, Queen Latifah was granted a temporary license to officiate the weddings in the state of California, which made the marriages legal and binding in the eyes of the law.

producer. In an interview with David Letterman, she exclaimed about the premise of her new talk show: "No more paternity tests!" in reference to some of the raunchy themes that prevail on daytime television. Instead she wanted to focus on positive human stories, which would include celebrity interviews, musical performances, sketch comedy, human-interest stories, and sincere discussions about current events.

Debuting in the fall of 2013, *The Queen Latifah Show* captivated audiences and became the best-rated new talk show since *Dr. Oz* in 2009. Already renewed for a second season, it received a People's Choice Award for Best New Talk Show, edging out shows hosted by Arsenio Hall, Jenny McCarthy, and Bethenny Frankel.

The Queen Latifah Show was an instant success—and is a much more rewarding experience for Dana than her first talk show.

Latifah's Legacy

Dana Owens wants every girl and woman to realize that inside them lives a queen—not a princess who is spoiled and demanding, but a queen who is wise and conducts herself with dignity. A queen is diplomatic, makes no enemies, and remembers those who were loyal to her. A queen knows her strength and isn't afraid to use it.

Through fame, fortune, tragedy, and success, she remains a loving daughter and faithful friend to the people who knew her when she was just "Dana from around the way." From apartment 3K of the Hyatt Court housing projects in Newark to her luxury home in the Hollywood Hills, she has embraced every leg of her heroic odyssey. Long live the queen.

Queen Latifah

Timeline

1978
Parents separate; moves with mother and brother to Hyatt Court housing projects

1987
Graduates Irvington High School; attends Borough of Manhattan Community College; cuts her first demo

1992
Brother, Winki, dies in motorcycle crash

1970
Born in Newark, New Jersey, on March 18

1980
Leaves Hyatt Court

1991
Releases second album, *Nature of a Sistah*

Chooses the name "Latifah"
1978

Leads her high school basketball team to the state championship
1984

Appears in *Jungle Fever*
1991

Skips a grade at school
1979

Releases first album, *All Hail the Queen*
1989

2006

Unveils star on the Hollywood Walk of Fame, making her the first hip-hop singer to do so

2014

Officiates the marriage of thirty-three straight, gay and interracial couples at the Grammys

1999

Stars in her own talk show

1993

Releases third album, *Black Reign*; wins first Grammy Award

2003

Nominated for Academy Award for her role in *Chicago*

2013

The Queen Latifah Show premieres

Publishes first book *Ladies First: Revelations of a Strong Woman*

Releases first non-rap album, *The Dana Owens Album*

Performs "America the Beautiful" during Super Bowl XXVIII

1999

2004

2014

Stars in sitcom *Living Single*

Lands CoverGirl endorsement

Publishes second book, *Put on Your Crown: Life-Changing Moments on the Path to Queendom*

1993

2001

2010

SOURCE NOTES

Chapter 1

P. 5, Queen Latifah, *Ladies First: Revelations of a Strong Woman* (New York: William Morrow, 1999), p. xi.

P. 9, Queen Latifah, *Put on Your Crown: Life-Changing Moments on the Path to Queendom* (New York: Grand Central Publishing, 2010), p. 98.

P. 12, Queen Latifah, *Ladies First: Revelations of a Strong Woman*, p. 27

P. 16, Queen Latifah, *Put on Your Crown: Life-Changing Moments on the Path to Queendom*, p. 26.

P. 16, Queen Latifah, *Put on Your Crown: Life-Changing Moments on the Path to Queendom*, p. 44.

Chapter 2

P. 21, Queen Latifah, *Ladies First: Revelations of a Strong Woman*, p. 6.

P. 24, Queen Latifah, *Ladies First: Revelations of a Strong Woman*, p. 17.

Chapter 3

P. 39, Lawrence, Rebecca, "Forty Years On From the Party Where Hip Hop Was Born," www.bbc.com/culture/story/20130809-the-party-where-hip-hop-was-born.

Chapter 4

P. 46, Queen Latifah, *Ladies First: Revelations of a Strong Woman*, p. 53.

P. 53, Queen Latifah, *Ladies First: Revelations of a Strong Woman*, p. 64.

Chapter 5

P. 59, Queen Latifah, *Put on Your Crown: Life-Changing Moments on the Path to Queendom*, p. 68.

P. 65, Henderson, Alex, "Queen Latifah: All Hail the Queen Review," www.allmusic.com.

P. 65, Christgrau, Robert, "Queen Latifah: All Hail the Queen Review," www.allmusic.com.

Chapter 6

P. 74, Queen Latifah, *Put on Your Crown: Life-Changing Moments on the Path to Queendom*, p. 138.

P. 75, Queen Latifah, *Put on Your Crown: Life-Changing Moments on the Path to Queendom*, p. 93.

P. 76, Queen Latifah, *Ladies First: Revelations of a Strong Woman*, p. 92.

P. 76, Queen Latifah, *Put on Your Crown: Life-Changing Moments on the Path to Queendom*, p. 144.

Chapter 7

P. 87, Queen Latifah, *Put on Your Crown: Life-Changing Moments on the Path to Queendom*, p. 36.

P. 92, Queen Latifah, *Put on Your Crown: Life-Changing Moments on the Path to Queendom*, p. 187.

P. 93, Queen Latifah, *Put on Your Crown: Life-Changing Moments on the Path to Queendom*, p. 187.

P. 93, Queen Latifah, *Put on Your Crown: Life-Changing Moments on the Path to Queendom*, p. 1.

P. 95, Gelt, Jessica, "Grammys 2014: Queen Latifah on Her Role in the 'Same Love' Wedding," *Los Angeles Times*, January 27, 2014.

P. 95, Runice, Charlotte, "Grammys 2014: Queen Latifah Officiates 33 Marriages," *The Telegraph*, January 27, 2014.

P. 95, "The Late Show: Queen Latifah Talks 'Teach,'" www.cbs.com.

GLOSSARY

AIDS Acquired immune deficiency syndrome; a virus that attacks an infected individual's cellular immunity, increasing their chances of infection by other disease.

apartheid The South African policy of racial segregation.

Black Power A movement based on racial pride that was especially prominent in the 1960s and 70s and that demanded rights for black people.

certified gold A designation in the music business that denotes a song or album has sold more than 500,000 units.

civil rights movement The mass popular movement that reached its peak in the 1950s and '60s that sought to secure basic privileges and equal access to opportunities for African Americans.

demo A rough recording of a song not intended for wide release; musicians seeking to secure a contract with a record label will sometimes forward a demo to executives to illustrate their style and message.

dialect A form or manner of language that is unique to a region or social group.

DJ (disc jockey) An individual who mixes recorded music.

exodus A mass departure of people at the same time.

hip-hop A style of music that originated with black and Hispanic youth during the 1970s and features rap with electronic backing.

housing project A government-sponsored residential development with controlled rents.

Jim Crow laws A series of laws that enforced racial segregation in the South between the end of the formal Reconstruction period in 1877 and the beginning of a strong civil rights movement in the 1950s; based on the premise of "separate but equal," in practice facilities reserved for black citizens were inferior to those for whites.

Ku Klux Klan (KKK) Either of two distinct U.S. hate organizations that have employed terror in pursuit of their white supremacist agenda; one group was founded immediately after the Civil War and lasted until the 1870s, the other began in 1915 and has continued to the present.

MC (master of ceremonies) A term used to describe a rapper who uses prewritten or spontaneous rhymes to introduce DJs.

mecca A place that attracts people with a particular interest.

misogynistic The hatred of women.

music label A business that manages the production, manufacturing, distribution, marketing, and promotion for copyrighted music recordings and music videos; also called a "record label" or "label."

National Association for the Advancement of Colored People (NAACP) An interracial American organization created to work for the abolition of segregation and discrimination in housing, education, employment, voting, and transportation and to ensure African Americans their constitutional rights; created in 1909.

posthumous Occurring after death.

producer A person who oversees a musical recording, usually by determining the overall sound.

promoter A person who finances or organizes a musical performance.

scene A particular area of interest or activity; a subculture.

social mobility The movement of individuals or groups in social hierarchy, most commonly based on economics.

solidarity Unity with or within a particular group.

FURTHER INFORMATION

Books

Baker, Soren. *The History of Rap and Hip-hop*. Music Library. Farmington Hills, MI: Lucent Books, 2006.

Queen Latifah. *Ladies First: Revelations of a Strong Woman*. New York: William Morrow, 1999.

Queen Latifah. *Put on Your Crown: Life-Changing Moments on the Path to Queendom*. New York: Grand Central Publishing, 2010.

Websites

The Queen Latifah Show
queenlatifah.com
Watch videos of interviews, view photos of Latifah and guests, listen to music performance recordings, discover new recipes, and read Queen Latifah's fashion blog.

Queen Latifah on Twitter
twitter.com/IAMQUEENLATIFAH
Stay up-to-date with all things "Queen." Check out behind-the-scenes photos from *The Queen Latifah Show* and discover what's new with Queen Latifah.

BIBLIOGRAPHY

Biography.com. "Queen Latifah." Accessed April 3, 2014. www.biography.com/people/queen-latifah-9542419.

Bonelli, Winnie. "N.J.'s Fun-Loving Queen Latifah Making an Impact with Her TV Show." *New Jersey Newsroom*, December 27, 2013.

CBS.com. "The Late Show: Queen Latifah Talks 'Teach.'" Accessed April 3, 2014. www.cbs.com/shows/late_show/video/61Fu6HkmWJTOnwROVanekNfp85fomLZO/david-letterman-queen-latifah-on-her-cbs-special-teach-.

Dandy, Brittany. "Queen Latifah Transcends Hip-Hop for Rock Star Honors." MTV.com, November 3, 2013.

HHE. "Flavor Unit Entertainment Launches Flavor Unit Records and Gears Up for Their First Release." October 4, 2002.

James, Meg. "'The Queen Latifah Show' Turns in Solid Debut." *Los Angeles Times*, September 17, 2013.

Keeps, David A. "Queen Latifah on Surviving Her Darkest Moment—And Finding Joy." *Good Housekeeping*, December 2013.

Law Library. "Black Power Movement." Accessed April 3, 2014. law.jrank.org/pages/4776/Black-Power-Movement.html.

McKynzie, Amber. "Queen Latifah Decoded: The Grammy-Winning Rapper Turns into a CoverGirl." *Black Enterprise*, December 31, 2012.

"Newark Riots—1967." *Rutgers*, Accessed April 3, 2014. www.67riots.rutgers.edu/n_index.htm.

NPR.org. "Queen Latifah on New HBO Movie 'Life Support.'" March 9, 2007.

PBS.org. "Newark: A Brief History." POV, July 5, 2005.

QueenLatifah.com. *The Queen Latifah Show*.

Queen Latifah. *Ladies First: Revelations of a Strong Woman*. New York, NY: William Morrow, 1999.

Queen Latifah. *Put on Your Crown: Life-Changing Moments on the Path to Queendom*. New York, NY: Grand Central Publishing, 2010.

Snyder, Gail. *Hip-hop: Queen Latifah*. Broomall, PA: Mason Crest Publishers, 2007.

INDEX

ABOUT THE AUTHOR

Amy Pettinella is an author, music promoter, and playwright living in Indianapolis, Indiana. She runs an intimate concert salon for indie artists and poets called Beat Lounge. An active reporter of local arts and national music, she regularly reviews art and music for *Mission Intrigue: Indy* and *No Depression Roots Music Authority*.